ISBN 978-1-330-47194-4
PIBN 10066245

1 MONTH OF
FREE
READING

at

www.ForgottenBooks.com

By purchasing this book you are eligible for one month membership to ForgottenBooks.com, giving you unlimited access to our entire collection of over 1,000,000 titles via our web site and mobile apps.

To claim your free month visit:

www.forgottenbooks.com/free66245

English
Français
Deutsche
Italiano
Español
Português

www.forgottenbooks.com

Mythology Photography **Fiction**
Fishing Christianity **Art** Cooking
Essays Buddhism Freemasonry
Medicine **Biology** Music **Ancient**
Egypt Evolution Carpentry Physics
Dance Geology **Mathematics** Fitness
Shakespeare **Folklore** Yoga Marketing
Confidence Immortality Biographies
Poetry **Psychology** Witchcraft
Electronics Chemistry History **Law**
Accounting **Philosophy** Anthropology
Alchemy Drama Quantum Mechanics
Atheism Sexual Health **Ancient History**
Entrepreneurship Languages Sport
Paleontology Needlework Islam
Metaphysics Investment Archaeology
Parenting Statistics Criminology
Motivational

SAVOURIES À LA MODE

BY

MRS DE SALIS

FOURTEENTH EDITION

'Anchovies and Sack'—Shakespeare

LONDON

LONGMANS, GREEN, AND CO.

AND NEW YORK : 15 EAST 16th STREET

1894

PREFACE.

SAVOURY DISHES at the present time being so fashionable, and novelties in them so much inquired for, I have been persuaded by my friends to publish a small book on the subject. Many of the recipes are new, a few original, and I trust all will be found welcome. I have endeavoured to give all the recipes in as practical a manner as possible, so that any plain cook could manage them, at all events after one or two trials, and with a few hints from her mistress. And as I am glad to know that in these days of Schools of Cookery many mistresses have become their own *chefs*, bad cooking in an establishment should be a thing of the past.

HARRIET A. DE SALIS.

SAVOURIES À LA MODE.

Anchovy Canapés.

Les Canapés aux Anchois.

Cut some slices of crumb of bread a quarter of an inch thick, cut these in pieces two-and-a-half inches long, one-and-a-half inch wide, and fry them in clarified butter till of a nice golden colour ; when cold, spread these slices with anchovy butter. Steep some anchovies in cold water, drain, open, and trim them. Place four fillets of anchovies on each piece of bread, leaving three small spaces between the fillets ; fill the first space with chopped hard-boiled white of egg, fill the middle space with chopped parsley, and the third with chopped hard-boiled yolk of egg rubbed through the sieve.

Anchovy Creams.

Crèmes d'Anchois.

Take some of Cunningham and Fourrier's pâte d'anchois, mix it with some thick cream into which half a pint of aspic jelly has been mixed, add some carmine till the mixture becomes a pretty salmon colour, wet some little dariole moulds into which

B

lobster coral has been sprinkled ; put in the anchovy mixture and let stand on ice for a couple of hours ; turn out and garnish with chopped aspic and chervil leaves.

Anchovy and Olive Straws.
Pailles aux Olives et Anchois.

Take twelve French olives, stone them and mince them finely, rub them through a sieve and let them dry ; take six anchovies, scrape and bone them, pound them in a mortar and pass them through the sieve, then mix them with the olives. Take two ounces of butter and the anchovy mixture and rub well into two ounces of Vienna flour, thoroughly mix, add the yolk of an egg and make all into a stiff paste. Roll the paste out the same as for cheese straws, and cut them into lengths the same way, and bake in a hot oven for ten minutes, the heat rising to 246°.

Anchovy Straws.
Pailles d'Anchois.

Take two ounces of flour and mix with it a little salt and a *cayenne*-spoonful of coralline pepper. Then take two ounces of anchovies that have been washed, boned, pounded, and passed through a sieve. Rub the anchovy paste and two ounces of butter well into the flour, then mix all these ingredients together with the yolk of an egg to a smooth paste. Roll the paste out into a strip $\frac{1}{8}$ of an inch in thickness and 5 inches wide. Cut this paste, with a sharp knife dipped in flour, into strips $\frac{1}{8}$ of an inch wide, so that the straws will be 5 inches long and $\frac{1}{8}$ of *an inch in* thickness.

Put these on to a baking sheet and put them into a *hot* oven for ten minutes, the heat rising to 246°. Dish them up cross-bar fashion, and send them to table *hot.* Cod's roe can be used instead of anchovies, making cod's-roe straws.

Stuffed Anchovies.

Anchois Farcis.

Split open six anchovies, wash them in Chablis or some white wine, then bone them.

Mix some chopped fish, bread-crumbs, and yolks of eggs together ; stuff the anchovies with these, dip them into batter and fry. Garnish with fried parsley.

Canapés à la Crème.

Cut little rounds of bread, fry them a pale colour, curl some washed and boned anchovies and place on them, and pour over either Devonshire or whipped cream.

Anchovies à la Melhonaise.

Make some toast, cut it into neat square pieces, butter it liberally, and spread it very thickly with the following mixture :—

Stir in a gallipot (placed in a saucepan of hot water over the fire) the beaten yolk of one egg, one ounce of butter, two teaspoonfuls of anchovy paste (Cunningham and Fourrier's pâte aux anchois is best), a teaspoonful of mushroom ketchup, six olives finely pounded, and a gill of cream, until it becomes the thickness of rich custard. It must not be allowed to boil. Whip a gill of cream to a froth, let it drain awhile on a sieve, then pile it up on each piece of toast over the anchovy custard. Fillet and bone some anchovies (which should have been soaked in milk), cut the fillets into halves, lay four strips against the piled-up cream on each square of toast, the ends meeting at the top. Place in refrigerator and serve iced.

Anchovy Fingers.

Prepare some croûtons cut in finger lengths slightly hollowed, and lay in each a washed and boned anchovy fillet and flakes of smoked salmon. Garnish with thick mayonnaise sauce and chopped capers.

Anchovy Toast à Champagne.

Mix over the fire one ounce of butter with the well-beaten yolks of two eggs, a teaspoonful of essence of anchovy and one of champagne. When quite hot and thick (it must not boil) pour it on some rather thick slices of hot toast and set it in the oven for two or three minutes to soak, and serve very hot.

Bloater Roes with Oysters.

Cut some pieces of bread three inches long and one wide, half-an-inch deep, hollow out the centre and fry quite crisp ; fill with soft roes of bloaters with three oysters on each, which must be sautéd in butter for a couple of minutes ; add a squeeze of lemon, a sprinkling of cayenne, and serve very hot. *Fresh* herring roes can be so used.

Canapés à la Bismarck.

Cut some rounds of bread with a two-inch cutter, fry them a light brown ; spread over each some anchovy butter, then curl round on each an anchovy well washed and trimmed ; sprinkle over them olives very finely shred.

Caviar Canapés.

Cut some slices of crumb of bread a quarter of an inch thick ; cut them out with a plain two-inch cutter, and fry these rounds in a little clarified butter till of a light golden colour. When cold, spread them over with Montpelier butter and place a layer of caviar on the top. Squeeze lemon over them and serve.

Cod's Roe.

Laitances de Morue.

Take some smoked cod's roe, shave it into very small pieces, put it into a saucepan with a good-sized piece of butter and a little pepper ; stir it well over the fire, and pour it on pieces of toast cut in rounds. Sometimes muffin is used instead of toast.

Crab Savoury.

Take three tablespoonfuls of fine white bread-crumbs, one tablespoonful of melted butter, two tablespoonfuls of tarragon vinegar, one teaspoonful of chili vinegar, three of cream, one teaspoonful of salt, half a teaspoonful of made mustard, and a dust of cayenne pepper.

Carefully remove all the *edible* meat from the

body and claws; take care to put away the stomach and any greenish matter. Take the yolk of an egg and mix it with the salt, mustard, cayenne, and melted butter, and when thoroughly mixed add gradually the vinegars, next the bread crumbs and crab, lastly stir in the cream lightly and turn the mixture into little paper or china ramekin dishes and garnish with chervil.

Croûtes à la Stanley.

Make little rounds of fried bread and place on them either some Devonshire or whipped cream and pour on to the croûtes with forcers, so that the cream stands up in a pyramid form ; cut some boned anchovies into *narrow* fillets and decorate the cream with them arranged like lattice-work.

Haddock Canapés.

Take the flesh of one small or half a large haddock, free from the bones, and pound it in a mortar with one ounce of butter. When fine, rub it through a coarse sieve and stir it over the fire with a little cream and a dust of coralline pepper till quite hot, then pour it on some neat pieces of hot buttered toast and serve quickly.

Dried Haddock Rissoles.

Lay the haddock in a frying-pan, cover it with boiling water and boil it for a few minutes, then drain it, remove the flesh, pound it in a mortar, mix *with it a little* grated Parmesan cheese, a little chopped parsley, a dust of coralline pepper, and one or two well-beaten eggs, according to the quantity of fish and cheese ; roll the mixture into tiny balls, fry them in butter, and serve them on croûtons of fried bread.

Dried Haddock and Tomatoes.

Soak a dried haddock for four hours, skin it and take away all bones and break the fish into flakes. Slice a small onion and two tomatoes, chop up a dessertspoonful of parsley, sprinkle with pepper and salt, and cook in an ounce of butter till quite soft, then add the fish and cook for ten minutes. Dish up on a border of boiled rice.

Finnan Haddock Balls.

Pound the fish well and mix it with butter, pepper, and a little cream, then make into very small rissoles with a few bread-crumbs and fry ; slices of brown bread and butter being served with them.

Fish Fritters (Smoked).

Make some batter, flake some smoked salmon (or bloaters), dust the pieces lightly with cayenne, dip in the batter, and fry till crisp *in oil*. Drain well, and serve piled up high and garnished with parsley.

Lobster in Aspic.

Aspic de Homard.

Make the jelly the same as under ' Aspic Jelly. Have some lobster cut in pieces, three eggs boiled hard, and a few pieces of tarragon and cress. Put a layer of the jelly in the mould, then arrange in designs pieces of the lobster alternately with the eggs, and here and there pieces of the green, according to fancy.

When this has all set, put in more lobster, &c., and then more jelly in a half-melted state, and so on till the entire mould is filled up ; sprinkling in here and there a little lobster coral. These aspic moulds can be varied in every possible form. They can be made with prawns, fish, game, eggs, pâté de foie gras, caviar, and mushrooms. Much depends on the taste of the *artiste* in their appearance : they can be ornamented with lobster coral, pistachio kernels chopped fine, yolks and hard-boiled whites of eggs cut into various devices. Barberries placed in the form of rings on the top make a very gay appearance ; or the top could be made in six sections—two of barberries, two of pistachio kernels, and two of rings of white of egg.

Chopped aspic, parsley, and slices of lemon should be garnished round the moulds, and they always look best served in a silver dish.

Lobster Bashaws.

Homard à la Turc.

Pick the meat from a large lobster, mince it finely, and pound it in a mortar with a little salt, pepper, cayenne, and butter ; divide the shell into quarters, scrape these thoroughly, and sprinkle over the inside some fine dried bread-crumbs. Put the mixture into the shells, cover thickly with bread-crumbs, pour over the top a quarter of a pound of *clarified* butter, an ounce over each quarter, and bake in a quick oven about ten minutes. Serve the meat in the shells, neatly arranged on a hot napkin, and garnish with bright green parsley.

Lobsters à la Bordelaise.

Homards à la Bordelaise.

Cut up two lobsters each into eight pieces ; break the claws without spoiling their shape, and boil for twenty-five minutes in white wine, seasoned with a head of garlic, a laurel leaf, a bouquet garni of parsley and herbs, pepper and salt ; place the cover on the saucepan and stir occasionally ; when done, dry each piece in a cloth and put them into a clean saucepan. Brown two sliced onions and shalots in butter, stir in a tablespoonful of flour, and when quite thick moisten with some of the liquor in which the lobsters were boiled ; stir over a quick fire for ten minutes ; add two tablespoonfuls of tomato sauce and a pinch of cayenne. Pour the sauce over the lobsters, and warm for a few moments. Dish up the pieces so arranged as to give the appearance of the lobsters not having been cut ; garnish with the claws ; cover with the sauce and serve.

Lobster Canapés.

Les Canapés aux Homards.

Cut and fry the bread as for caviar canapés ; spread the rounds with lobster butter and a lobster scallop previously soaked in oil, vinegar, salt, and pepper ; in the centre place a row of capers round the lobster, and serve.

Lobster Creams.

Homard en Ciel.

Take the flesh of a lobster, pound it well in the mortar with cream, rub it through a sieve; add an eggspoonful of anchovy sauce and beat it up well in a pound of Devonshire clotted cream; put this into the little French china ramequin moulds, strew coral over the top, and serve.

Gratin of Lobster.

Gratin de Homard.

Cut a good-sized lobster in half and pick out all the meat, which must be cut into thin slices. Put a piece of butter the size of an egg into a saucepan with three shalots finely minced. Brown them lightly, then mix in a tablespoonful of flour, and, when quite smooth, add half a pint of milk. Simmer for five minutes. Put in the sliced lobster, a tablespoonful of chopped parsley, a little salt and cayenne, and half a teaspoonful of anchovy sauce. Stir over the fire, and, when boiling, draw the saucepan back, and add the well-beaten yolk of an egg. Fill the shell of the lobster with the mixture, sprinkle bread-crumbs over it, and pour on a little clarified butter. Put the shell in a hot oven for twenty minutes, dish on a napkin, and serve.

Lobster Omelet.

Omelette au Homard.

This omelet is made like all the other omelets, *substituting* lobster in place of oysters, kidney, &c.

It can be made in two ways, exactly like the receipts given for oyster omelet. Sardines or anchovies may be used instead of lobster.

Small Rolls with Lobster.
Petits Pains à la Française au Homard.

Prepare the rolls as for chicken rolls, then cut some lobster tails into small dice. Mix them in some mayonnaise sauce with some chopped Montpelier butter. Fill the rolls, replace the covers, and serve.

These rolls may be made with game, prawns, or shrimps.

Lobster Salad en Mascarade.

Take a plain round mould and place a gallipot inside filled with cold water or ice. At the bottom of the mould first place a layer of nicely-flavoured aspic jelly coloured red, which has been whisked up ; when nearly set lay this on ice, and when set add a layer of natural-coloured aspic, also whisked up, then a layer of aspic coloured green, and so on till the mould is full. Put on ice till quite firm, then pour out the iced water from the gallipot and fill it with hot water and remove it ; then fill in the space with lobster mayonnaise, which of course has already been prepared. Place on ice again for an hour or so, and then turn out, garnish with aspic, slices of cucumber, prawns, &c.

Grilled Mackerel Bones.

Take the bones of a boiled mackerel, dust them with salt and cayenne pepper, and broil over a clear fire till crisp but not burnt. Serve with hot toast and butter. There must be as many bones as guests.

Prawns in Disguise.

Crevettes en Mascarade.

Cut some small rounds of bread and butter two inches in diameter, peel some prawns, marinade them in some mayonnaise sauce ; place three on each round of bread with a small piece of watercress on each, place over all some whipped aspic jelly ; strew lobster coral over them, and garnish with aspic jelly cut in the shape of lozenges.

Prince of Wales Canapés.

Canapés à la Prince de Galles.

Take some fine prawns, fillets of anchovies, celery, two gherkins, and two truffles. Cut all these into small squares, put them into a basin with enough Prince of Wales sauce to season the ingredients. Fill ramequin or china cases with this mixture, and lay a piece of aspic jelly on the top of each, garnishing with the same chopped.

Prince of Wales sauce for above : two yolks of eggs boiled hard, two anchovies, some tarragon, the latter parboiled and dried, a few capers, a little mustard, and the yolk of an egg. Bruise all these in a mortar, and then work in one tablespoonful of salad oil, a teaspoonful of tarragon vinegar, and rub through a sieve.

Angels on Horseback.

Anges à Cheval.

Take *very thin* slices of fat bacon, cut all the rind off. Then take an oyster (or two if very small), pour on it two drops of essence of anchovy, four of lemon, and a grain of cayenne, and roll it in the slice of bacon. When there are sufficient of these rolls, put them on a small skewer and fry them ; when cooked take each one separately and place on a fried croûton. This is a dish which must be served very hot.

Oyster Baskets à la Hartington.

Scoop out the interiors of some smooth tomatoes which have been cut in half, and drain them from juice. Take some large stewing oysters, cut them into dice, make a good white sauce with cream, flavour with the liquor from the oysters, a little cayenne and lemon juice. Fill the tomatoes with these. Take an anchovy that has been well soaked with milk, and cut it up small and lay on the top, and place parsley stalks across for the handle, dish on fried croûtons, and send up hot to table. Instead of the anchovy a little bacon chopped up makes a nice variety.

Oyster Omelet.

Omelette aux Huîtres.

Blanch and beard eight oysters and mince them finely with three drops of anchovy sauce. Then proceed the same as for kidney omelet.

Another way of making oyster omelet is to make a plain omelet, and after it is folded place in between the folds a tablespoonful of good oyster sauce and hold the salamander over it for a few seconds.

Prairie Oyster.

Put into a wine-glass a teaspoonful of vinegar, break a new laid egg into it, season with pepper and salt, and sprinkle it with vinegar and one drop of Worcester sauce.

Scalloped Oysters.

Coquilles aux Huîtres.

Open and beard a dozen oysters and scald them for a second in their own liquor.

Make a white sauce into which some oyster liquor is poured, a grain of cayenne, a saltspoonful of anchovy sauce, and a squeeze of lemon. Boil this till it is cooked.

Put the oysters in the scallop shell, pour the white sauce over them, and strew bread-crumbs on the top, and place some butter in small pieces all over.

Have the salamander red-hot, and brown them. Send them to table *very* hot.

Oyster Soufflé.

Soufflé aux Huîtres.

Take two dozen blue point oysters, mince them *and* rub them through a wire sieve. Blanch and

beard a dozen *large* oysters, and cut each one into
four pieces.

Put two ounces of flour and one ounce of butter
into a stewpan, and mix them well together over
the fire; then add a quarter of a pint of oyster
liquor, and stir all together till it thickens, and the
flour is well cooked. Put this sauce and the
pounded oysters into a mortar and pound them
well together, adding two yolks of eggs one at a
time, a little salt, cayenne pepper, and a quarter of
a pint of cream. When these are all thoroughly
mixed, beat three whites of egg to a stiff froth and
stir them into the mixture very lightly; then put
in the oysters. Butter the mould, pour in the
mixture, cover it with buttered paper and steam
it gently for half an hour. Strew lobster coral over
all.

Russian Tartlets.

Tartelettes à la Russe.

Make very light pastry tartlets; then take some
oysters boiled in their own liquor (cut off their
beards), one grated tablespoonful of horseradish,
one gill of stock, some lemon juice, one tablespoonful of vinegar, one gill of white sauce, one
teaspoonful of capers, half a gill of the oyster
liquor, and a very little salt; let all these boil a few
minutes. Then add, off the fire, the yolk of an
egg whisked up; now add the oysters. Then put
pieces of lobster, sardines, and anchovies at the
bottom of the tartlet cases, and fill up with the
oysters and sauce. Sprinkle over each, lobster
coral, parsley rubbed through a sieve, and capers.
Make hot in the oven for ten minutes, and serve.

Tartlets à l'Arlequin.

Take some tartlet pans, not too small—about the size of *small* mince-pie pans—and line them with puff paste. Roll round some of the paste into thin rolls, and put across the tartlets so as to make four divisions in two ; put anchovy cream mixture, which should be well smoothed over, and in the other two some lobster cream well coloured with lobster coral ; arrange the tartlets in a bed of chervil, and serve. Oyster cream may be used instead of the lobster cream if liked.

Devilled Sardines.

Mix together four tablespoonfuls of cold stock, one of chutney paste, one of ketchup, two of made mustard, one of salt, and two of butter. Mix very smoothly, then put the sardines into it, and stew gently till thoroughly warmed. Soak some thin captain's biscuits in sweet oil or clarified butter. Then rub each side well over with the above mixture and toast them on the gridiron over a clear fire ; then lift out each sardine separately, cut off the heads and tails, split open and bone, trim it to fit a biscuit, lay one on each, and brown with a salamander or before the fire. Serve quickly and very hot.

Dressed Sardines.

Croûtons à la Sardine.

Cut six bread croûtons two inches in diameter, fry them, and then make a mixture of two teaspoonfuls of essence of anchovy, two teaspoonfuls of Worcester sauce, a grain of cayenne, one dessertspoonful of flour, two ounces of butter, and a quarter pint of boiling water, which should simmer till the flour is well cooked. Scrape and bone six sardines, pound them in butter and put them on the croûtons ; then pour over the sauce, squeeze a few drops of lemon juice over, and serve.

Fisherman's Canapés.

Canapés ' al Pescatore.'

Cut rounds of bread ; fry them. Make fillets of sardines, oysters, lobster, &c., and lay them on the bread in strips across and across, and run butter round the edge in ornamental patterns. Montpelier butter can be used alternately with plain butter.

✗ ### Sardine Eggs.

Œufs aux Sardines.

Boil four eggs for ten minutes and put them into cold water ; scrape four sardines gently and pound them in the mortar.

Shell the eggs and cut them in half lengthways, take out the yolks and add them to the sardines in the mortar with one ounce of butter, a little white pepper and salt, and a dessert-spoonful of parsley. Pound all together ; then fill the whites and put the two halves together, and serve in a nest of small salad sprinkled with oil and vinegar.

Sardines à l'Indienne.

Place the yolks of four eggs in a stewpan with a pat of fresh butter, a spoonful of chutney, a little salt and cayenne to taste ; stir these ingredients over a slow fire till they form a fairly firm paste,

C

Carefully trim each sardine, and absorb their moisture with a fish cloth.

Thoroughly mask them with the mixture, egg and bread-crumb them, fry to a delicate hue in clarified butter ; dish them up on strips of thin crisp toast, and serve very hot.

Sardines Maître d'Hôtel.

Take six sardines, a dessert-spoonful of chopped parsley, one thin slice of onion pounded fine, one tablespoonful of chili vinegar, half a pint of melted butter, and a round of toast ; scrape the sardines, arrange them neatly on toast, and put the above sauce over them, adding a squeeze of lemon juice and cayenne to it.

Sardines à la Piémontaise.

Fry some bread in boiling lard or butter ; cut it into fingers ; scale and wipe some sardines, make them hot in the oven, and place one on each finger of bread ; then pour over them the following sauce :—The yolks of four eggs well whipped, half an ounce of butter, one teaspoonful of tarragon vinegar, one teaspoonful of common vinegar, a mustard-spoonful of made mustard, and a little salt. These must be well stirred over the fire till the sauce thickens but does not boil.

Savoury Canapés.

Brioches.

Take three tablespoonfuls of mayonnaise sauce, some celery very finely chopped, a small shalot well pounded, pieces of anchovies, lobster, sardines, oysters, and shrimps, a little tarragon and chervil finely minced ; mix the ingredients with the mayonnaise sauce, and fill the brioche cases (which are best bought) ; run butter through the forcer round the edge of the brioche cases. Stand them on Montpelier butter (butter and watercress, *see* under that heading), strew lobster coral and hard-boiled yolks passed through a sieve on the top of each ; serve with chopped aspic round. These brioche cases can be also filled with caviar.

Savoury Trifle.

Bouchées à la Lucullus.

Cut a thick slice of bread from a large stale loaf ; cut off the crust, hollow out the centre ; fry a pale brown, and drain on a sieve.

Fill the hollow with lobster or crab pulled finely. Place a bed of salad in an entrée dish, on which place the croustade or slice of bread filled with lobster ; pour over mayonnaise sauce, and **sprinkle** with lobster coral.

Scalloped Scallops.

Coquilles à l'Escalope.

Wash the scallops well in two or three waters, trim away the beards, preserving the white, black, and orange-coloured parts. Mince the scallops finely, and mix with them a very little finely chopped parsley and a little pepper, salt, and a trifle of cayenne. Make a white sauce, cook it well, add the squeeze of a lemon ; then throw the minced

C 2

scallops into the sauce for a second, give one turn
on the fire, and pour into the shells ; add six drops
of chili vinegar, strew bread-crumbs over, and
place on the top plenty of little pieces of butter ;
brown with the salamander, and serve very hot.

Shrimp Canapés.

Canapés aux Crevettes.

Cut and fry the bread as for caviar sandwiches ;
when cold, spread over with shrimp butter ; place
the picked shrimps on the top in the form of a
rosette, leaving a space in the middle for a little
chopped parsley.

Devilled Shrimps.

Take some fresh shrimps, shell them, roll them
in flour, and put them in a frying basket and fry
them in clean boiling fat till a nice golden colour
and quite crisp. Turn them then into a cloth which
has been well sprinkled with salt and cayenne
pepper, and toss them about, and serve as hot as
possible ; pile up like whitebait.

Shrimp Rolls.

Crevettes en Surprise.

Take French rolls, cut them into very thin
slices, butter them well ; place on them some
picked shrimps, curl the slices round ; dish up in a
pyramid garnished with small salad.

Shrimp Toast.
Crevettes à la Bonnefemme.

Mix in a saucepan the yolks of two eggs, one teaspoonful of anchovy sauce ; soak in this a thick round of buttered toast. Peel some shrimps and place them on the toast, and serve hot.

Eggs à la Baldwin.

Boil four or six eggs till quite hard, cut the whites into very small pieces. Make a rich thick cream sauce, into which add a little chopped parsley and a little cayenne and salt ; put in the pieces of white of egg and boil all up for one minute, and have ready the yolks rubbed through a coarse sieve ; place the white egg mixture into a dish, cover with the tammied yolk, and brown lightly with a salamander.

Baked Eggs.
Œufs au Miroir.

Spread a thick layer of fresh butter on a tin or fire-proof china dish, sprinkle with salt, and break the eggs carefully on to it, one at a time ; pour some cream over them, season with salt, pepper, and one grate of nutmeg ; place a few small lumps of butter over all, bake in the oven, and brown with a salamander.

Eggs with Brown Butter.
Œufs au Beurre Noir.

Brown two ounces of fresh butter in a pan but do not let it burn ; add one tablespoonful of picked

parsley that has been washed and dried. Turn
this out of the pan, return the pan to the stove
again, and when quite hot put in two tablespoonfuls
of French vinegar ; let this boil, and pour it on to
the butter and parsley.

Next butter a pan, break in fresh eggs, place
them gently into a moderate oven until the white
is just set and the yolks lightly cooked ; cut them
round with a cutter, leaving a quarter of an inch
around the yolk, and pour the hot sauce round it.

Eggs in Cases.

Œufs en Caisse.

Oil some small paper ramequin cases (unless
the white fire-proof china cases are used), put into
each a piece of butter the size of a nut, with a small
pinch of parsley, some pepper, salt, and a cayenne-
spoonful of cayenne.   Break an egg into each case,
add a teaspoonful of grated Parmesan and a sprinkling of baked bread-crumbs.   Put the cases in the
oven for about five minutes, and serve.

Caviar Eggs.

Boil some eggs hard, cut them in halves, slice
a small piece from either end so that they may
stand, take out the yolks, put them in a mortar
with a small piece of butter and some caviare (for
four eggs a tablespoonful of caviare), incorporate
them all well together, adding a dust of cayenne
and six drops of lemon juice ; then fill the eggs with
this, piling the mixture high in them, and dish them
up on small round sippets of fried brown bread, or

instead of the brown bread croûtons. White bread may be used spread with watercress butter.

The Epicure's Eggs.
Œufs à la Gourmet.

Prepare the eggs as for lobster or shrimp eggs (*see* those recipes, pages 20–25), pound with the yolks some grated tongue and ham, moisten with a little meat jelly or aspic, and fill the hard-boiled whites with this mixture. On the top of each cut beetroot in the form of leaves, and arrange them round with a small spray of dried parsley in the middle of each.

Eggs au Gratin.
Œufs au Gratin.

Cut some hard-boiled eggs in slices and lay them on a well-buttered dish with grated Parmesan cheese, black pepper, and a grate of nutmeg. Sprinkle some baked bread-crumbs over all, put the dish in the oven, and serve as soon as the contents begin to colour.

Forced Eggs in Aspic.
Œufs Farcis en Aspic.

Boil four eggs hard, cut them into halves, take out the yolks and put them in the mortar with a teaspoonful of chopped parsley, a teaspoonful of lemon thyme, a grate of nutmeg, a very little salt, and still less cayenne ; pound these ingredients together with an ounce of butter ; when smooth, fill the whites with this mixture, and make what is over into little balls.

Have some aspic jelly, pour some into a border mould ; when it is nearly set put alternately round the mould and on the jelly the stuffed whites and the egg balls alternately. Then fill up the mould with the aspic and set on ice.

Indian Eggs.

Œufs à l'Indienne.

Cut a small slice from each end of some hard-boiled eggs, and cut them into halves, the round way. Take out the yolks and pound them in a mortar and mix them well with a mixture made as follows : a heaped teaspoonful of good curry-powder, two ounces of butter, and a dessert-spoonful of essence of anchovy, well blended and cooked in a stewpan. Fill the eggs with this mixture, dish them up, garnished with watercress and rolled bread and butter.

Scalloped Eggs and Oysters.

Coquilles d'Œufs aux Huîtres.

Melt two ounces of fresh butter in a saucepan with salt, pepper, a grate of nutmeg, a dessert-spoonful of minced parsley, a teaspoonful of minced chives and morels ; well cook this mixture and scald four dozen oysters in their own liquor and then put oysters and liquor (which must be strained) into the mixture, and give one boil ; then add five or six hard-boiled eggs sliced.

Simmer over a gentle fire for a few minutes ; then pour this into scallop shells, sprinkle with fine bread-crumbs, lay small pieces of butter on the *top, and brown* with the salamander.

Shrimp Eggs.

Œufs aux Crevettes.

Prepare the eggs the same as for Indian eggs. Pick some shrimps, place them in the mortar, and pound them thoroughly with the hard-boiled yolks and two ounces of butter, a grain of cayenne, a teaspoonful of essence of shrimps or anchovy. When these ingredients are thoroughly well mixed and pounded, fill the whites with the mixture. Place a sprig of watercress in each egg, and garnish with small salad.

These eggs may be varied by filling them with prawns or lobster instead of the shrimps.

Parmesan Eggs.

Œufs au Parmesan.

Prepare the eggs as for Indian eggs, &c., and pound with the yolks in a mortar two ounces of butter and two ounces of grated Parmesan cheese. Fill the whites, and garnish with small tomatoes in a circle around.

Scrambled Eggs and Tomatoes.

Œufs et Tomates à la Hâte.

Free from pips a large tomato, mince finely with two slices of Spanish onion, add plenty of butter, and pepper and salt to taste ; stir it in a stewpan on the fire till the onion is quite cooked but not coloured, then throw in four eggs beaten up, and keep on stirring the whole till the eggs are nearly set. Serve at once within a circle of fried bread sippets.

This can be made with Parmesan cheese instead of tomatoes.

Stuffed Eggs with Cream.

Œufs Farcis à la Crème.

Shell some hard-boiled eggs, cut them in half lengthways ; take out the yolks. Take an equal weight of butter with the yolks, and pound them, with a piece of bread-crumb the size of a small potato soaked in milk, in a mortar. Season with a grate of nutmeg, a grain of cayenne, a teaspoonful each of finely chopped parsley and shalot, a little salt, and three raw yolks of eggs. When well pounded pass through a sieve ; then fill the empty whites of egg with this mixture and pour some white or béchamel sauce made with thick cream over them.

Stuffed Eggs à la Provençale.

Œufs Farcis à la Provençale.

Take four hard-boiled eggs, shell them and cut them in half longways ; remove the yolks and put them into a mortar with three anchovies boned, two ounces of watercress, some butter, one teaspoonful of essence of anchovy, and a grain of cayenne. Pound all these ingredients well together, after which rub them through a hair sieve. Fill the whites with this mixture. Make small handles of parsley-stalks across the tops. Dish up on shredded lettuce, with the remainder of the mixture in the centre, and a little mayonnaise sauce poured over.

Swiss Eggs.

Œufs à la Suisse.

Spread two ounces of good butter on the bottom of a dish, and lay on it six thin slices of Gruyère cheese ; break six eggs upon this, keeping the yolks whole. Sprinkle over some mignonette pepper and salt. Mix a teaspoonful of chopped parsley and two ounces of grated Gruyère cheese together, and strew over them. Bake in a very quick oven for about ten or twelve minutes.

Eggs and Tomatoes.

Œufs à l'Espagnole.

Bake and skin tomatoes, cut them up and pass through a hair sieve. Put an ounce of butter into a stewpan, having rubbed the bottom slightly with garlic ; whilst it is getting hot over the fire, put in the tomatoes with a dessertspoonful of chopped onions and two capsicums. Beat up three eggs, add them to the tomatoes with salt and pepper to taste, keep stirring till nearly dry, when they are done, and should be dished up in the form of a pyramid.

Cheese Aigrettes.

Aigrettes au Parmesan.

Put one ounce of butter into half a pint of cold water till it boils ; when boiling add two-and-a-half ounces of *Vienna* flour, stirring vigorously all the time over the fire until it is cooked—that is to say, until the panado leaves the sides of the saucepan quite clean and coats the spoon. Take it off the fire, and when slightly cooled add two *whole* eggs and the yolk of another one by one, a little salt and cayenne, and then three ounces of Parmesan cheese grated, and beat well together. Have ready some fat not quite boiling, and drop small pieces of the mixture from a teaspoon and fry till a nice brown ; it generally takes five to ten minutes. Serve on a napkin in the form of a pyramid, and sprinkle with Parmesan cheese.

Baked Cheese.

Gruyère au Four.

Warm four ounces of butter in a quarter of a pint of water, add a saltspoonful of salt. As soon as this boils, stir in seven ounces of flour ; after a few minutes, take the saucepan off the fire, and add four yolks of eggs, the whites well whipped, and four ounces of grated Gruyère cheese ; pour this mixture into a china fireproof dish, cover it all over with very thin slices of the cheese, glaze with yolks of egg, and bake for twenty-five minutes.

Cheese Biscuits à la Saint-Denis.

Talmouses à la Saint-Denis.

Take three tablespoonfuls of fine flour, half a pound of cream curds, five ounces of Brie cheese which has been carefully scraped, and a pinch of salt ; pound all in a mortar ; then add five ounces of melted butter ; stir in three eggs to make a stiff paste, which must be rolled very thin, and cut into small round biscuits.

Bake in a quick oven and serve hot.

Cheese Balls.

Beat the whites of two eggs to a stiff froth, stir in two ounces of grated Parmesan cheese, salt and cayenne to taste ; shape the mixture into balls the size of marbles, and drop them into boiling fat. Fry them for five minutes till of a golden brown, drain well, and sprinkle grated cheese over them.

Kluskis of Cream Cheese.
Kluskis au Fromage à la Crème.

Take half a pound of fresh butter, six eggs, six tablespoonfuls of cream cheese, a pinch of powdered sugar, salt, and sufficient grated bread-crumbs and cream to make a paste ; mix well together, and roll into balls ; poach them in boiling salt and water, drain, and serve them with poivrade sauce.

Cheese Muff.

Take one-and-a-half ounces of butter, four ounces of grated cheese, one teaspoonful of salt, four well-beaten eggs. Put the cheese and butter and a few bread-crumbs into a saucepan over the fire ; when they begin to melt add the eggs and the seasoning ; stir and cook till the mixture can be pushed up into a soft muff-like form ; serve at once and quickly.

Cheese Omelet.
Omelette au Fromage.

Break three eggs into a basin and whip them till well mixed, add pepper, salt, and two ounces of grated Parmesan cheese.

Melt one ounce of butter in the omelet pan ; when the butter is quite hot pour the egg mixture into the pan, stir quickly to prevent sticking. Keep shaking the pan to prevent the omelet from sticking or burning ; spread it over the bottom of the pan to let it cook through, and watch it very carefully. When just set, take a knife and put it under the omelet and fold the omelet over. When the omelet is of a pale brown colour, turn it out of the pan into a hot dish.

Cheese Ramequins. •

Ramequins au Fromage.

Crumble a small stale roll and cover it with a breakfastcupful of milk, which must be quite boiling ; after it has *well* soaked, strain and put it in the mortar with four ounces of Parmesan and four ounces of Gloucester cheese grated, four ounces of fresh butter, half a teaspoonful of made mustard, a little salt and pepper, and a saltspoonful of sifted sugar. These ingredients must be all well pounded together with the yolks of four eggs, adding the well-whipped whites of the eggs. Half fill the paper cases or china moulds with this, bake them in a quick oven about ten to fifteen minutes, and serve hot as possible.

Cheese Soufflé.

Soufflé au Parmesan.

Mix a teaspoonful of flour very smoothly with half a pint of milk, a little salt and pepper ; simmer the mixture over the fire, stirring all the time, till *it is as thick* as melted butter ; stir into this about eight ounces of Parmesan or Gruyère cheese (the latter is best). Turn it into a basin, and mix with the yolks of four well-beaten eggs. Whisk the whites to a solid froth, and just before the soufflé is baked put them into it, and pour the mixture into a soufflé dish, which should only be half filled.

Time to bake, twenty minutes to half an hour.

Cheese Straws.
Pailles au Parmesan.

Take two ounces of flour, and mix with it a little salt and a *cayenne*-spoonful of red pepper. Then take three ounces of Parmesan cheese ; grate it. Rub the cheese and two ounces of butter well into the flour, then mix all these ingredients, together with the yolk of an egg, into a smooth stiff paste. Roll the paste out into a strip one-eighth of an inch in thickness and five inches wide, which is to be the length of the cheese straws. Cut this strip of paste into strips one-eighth of an inch wide, so that they will be five inches long and one-eighth of an inch in thickness. With the remainder of the paste, and with two round cutters, cut little rings of paste. Put the cheese straws and rings on the baking sheet and put them into a hot oven for ten minutes, the heat rising to 246°. For serving, put the cheese straws through the rings like a bundle of sticks.

Parmesan Creams.

Take some little dariole moulds and chemise them with aspic. Arrange some truffles cut into small shapes and in different devices and set in the jelly. Put on the ice, and when set put in the following mixture : Two ounces of Parmesan cheese finely grated, a dust of cayenne, salt to taste ; stir into this half a pint of double cream. Fill the moulds with this, stand on ice, and when cold turn out and serve garnished with very *small smooth* tomatoes placed between mounds of chopped aspic with sprays of chervil leaves.

Adelaide Sandwiches.
Tartines à l'Adelaïde.

Cut the breast of a fowl or of some game into very small dice ; wash four anchovies and cut them likewise into.dice and place them with the meat. Then put two spoonfuls of béchamel sauce and a small quantity of grated Parmesan, a little salt and cayenne, into a stewpan, stirring till reduced to a thick sauce ; then add the meat and anchovies. Mix the whole together and use the preparation as follows :—Cut two dozen croûtons in the form of a circle, fry them in clarified butter to a bright colour, and place one half on a clean baking sheet ; spread a thick layer of the above preparation on each of the croûtons, then cover them with the remaining twelve croûtons. Grate four ounces of Parmesan cheese and mix this with a pat of butter ; divide it into twelve parts and cover the top of each sandwich. About ten minutes before serving put them in the oven to be thoroughly warmed ; pass the red-hot salamander over them to colour them a bright yellow ; garnish with fried parsley.

Aspic Jelly.

Take a tablespoonful of Liebig, put two quarts *of water to it,* adding shalots, celery seed, thyme, two bay leaves, a carrot, turnip, and an onion stuck with cloves; let all simmer till it is all well impregnated with the vegetables. Then add the rind of a lemon cut thin, a glass of sherry, a few drops of chili vinegar, and a dessertspoonful of tarragon.

Put a large tablespoonful of gelatine with two of water, let it swell, then stir it in with the stock till it is dissolved; add the whites of two eggs slightly beaten up, and let all boil up; remove to side of fire and let it simmer for half an hour; then strain through a hot jelly-bag till clear, and pour it into a mould and place on ice.

Aspic Jelly à la Neptune.

Make the aspic jelly in the usual way and colour it *a very pale green*; have some little fish moulds and make a mixture of lobster and cream into which some aspic has been mixed; powder well with lobster coral, and sprinkle over some a little gold leaf and on others a little silver leaf, and then put some of the gold leaf into some of the fish moulds and the silver into another and put on ice for some hours to get *well iced*. In the meantime put some of the green aspic into the top of a fancy jelly mould and let it get set. When the fish moulds are ready to turn out, put in one or two, then some more of the green jelly and let set, and then more fish and jelly till the mould is full. Put on ice, and when ready turn out and garnish pale aspic chopped, and on which with a forcer put some lobster coral here and there in the form of sprays of coral.

D

Devilled Biscuits.

Biscuits à l'Enfer.

Take some water biscuits two-and-a-half inches in diameter, butter them on both sides, and pepper them well with black pepper and a little salt. Toast them before the fire or put them in the oven.

Or lay a mixture of cheese and made mustard on the biscuits and grill them.

Russian Biscuits.

Biscuits à la Russe.

Take some small thin captain's biscuits, mince finely cucumber, watercress, the white and yolk of a hard-boiled egg, and some anchovies well washed and dried. Cover each biscuit with this mixture ; place two or three capers in the middle, and garnish with aspic and watercress.

Egyptian Creams.

Make a purée of ham and curry powder well cooked. Have ready some of Cunninghame and Fourrier's pâté de foie gras, also the pâté aux anchois by the same maker ; have some little long-shaped paper cases the same as those sold for Neapolitan ices, put a layer of the ham and curry into them, and put it on ice, then a layer of the pâté de foie gras, then the anchovy, till the cases are full, and smooth some Montpelier butter on the top, and sprinkle with chopped aspic jelly, and *keep on ice* till ready.

Canapés à l'Exmoor.

Cut little rounds of bread, fry them a pale colour, curl some boned anchovies on them, and pour over all either Devonshire or whipped cream.

Canapés à la Rothschild.

Cut small rounds of bread, fry them a pale colour. Have some marrow, mix some cut truffles with it, make it *very* hot ; pour on the bread in a small conical shape, and curl a boned anchovy round on the top. Garnish with parsley, and serve **very** hot and quickly.

Chicken Rolls.
Petits Pains à la Française au Salpicon.

Take some French rolls, rasp them, cut out a piece of the crust on the top and remove the crumb from the inside. Prepare a mince of fillets of chicken, tongue, and truffles stirred into mayonnaise sauce.

Fill the rolls with this *salpicon,* replace the covers and dish them up.

Grenada Toasts.

Cut some fat and lean bacon into dice ; give them a few turns over the fire with parsley, onion, pepper, salt, and the yolks of two eggs. Stir it frequently till it forms a kind of forcemeat ; spread it over slices of bread cut of an equal thickness, and fry them.

Gnocchi à la Lombardy.

(Italian recipe.)

Boil one pound of potatoes, skin and mash them and pass them through a sieve ; then take half a pound of fine flour, add to the potatoes, and incorporate well together till an equal and consistent paste is made ; then divide it into pieces as large as a lemon and roll them on a board with the palms of the hands and form them into little sticks the size of walnuts ; then mould them one by one with the fingers into any desired shapes ; they must then be left to dry by leaving them exposed to the air on a drainer. In the meanwhile, put a saucepan on the fire with salted water, and when it boils throw in the gnocchi, a few at a time, till cooked ; then drain and season to taste ; arrange them on a dish with grated Parmesan cheese, and pour over melted butter and fried bacon.

Curry Toast.

Wash and bone half a dozen of anchovies, mix them with a little paste, a little mustard, some butter, and a few drops of chili vinegar ; spread the mixture on hot buttered toast, set it before the fire to heat. Serve very hot.

Fancy Savoury.

Fry some croûtons. They must be a nice square shape. Stone an olive and stand it on the centre of each. Curl a boned anchovy round it, and on two corners of the croûton place little heaps of finely cut hard-boiled egg, and on the other two *little piles of* lobster coral.

Iced Savoury Soufflé.

This dish can be made of almost any kind of fish, chicken, or game; it is excellent with crab. Cut up the crab, or whatever it may be, into very small pieces; let it soak in mayonnaise sauce for two or three hours. Have some well-flavoured aspic jelly and whip it till it is frothy. Put some of this at the bottom of the dish it is to be served in, then place a layer of the crab, and fill it up with aspic and crab alternately till the mould is nearly full; place a stiff band of paper round, and fill in with whipped aspic. Put it on ice for two hours, take off the paper, and serve.

Kidney Toast.
Tartines aux Rognons.

Split kidneys in two, remove sinews and outer skin, mince them finely. Put some chopped parsley and a little shalot also chopped into a stewpan with a little butter; let all fry together for a few moments. When done, add a tablespoonful of Worcester sauce, sprinkle in a very little flour, and boil up again for two minutes, so that the flour may be well cooked. Whilst boiling, stir in the minced kidneys with salt and pepper to taste.

Butter some thin slices of toast, cover them with the mince, and over that a thick layer of breadcrumbs mixed with a small quantity of Parmesan cheese; place them in a quick oven for ten minutes and serve very hot.

Kidney Omelet.
Omelette aux Rognons.

Take a sheep's kidney, cut it up into small pieces and sauté it in a stewpan with a little pepper and salt, a teaspoonful of parsley, and a small shalot chopped very fine. Beat the whites and yolks of three eggs separately ; mix the kidney and chopped shalot with the yolks of egg. Melt one-and-a-half ounce of butter in the pan, and make it very hot. Now stir the whipped whites into the yolks and put the mixture into the omelet-pan for two or three minutes over the fire, stirring all the time, and folding it as in the cheese omelet recipe.

Macaroni à l'Italienne.

Take a piece of gravy beef, cut in small pieces, put it into a stewpan with a sliced onion and a piece of butter ; toss it on the fire till the onion and the pieces of meat are browned, then add a glass of Chablis, a bunch of sweet herbs, a sliced carrot, pepper and salt to taste, a few mushrooms and tomatoes cut up, and a good allowance either of stock or tomato sauce.

Let the whole simmer for a couple of hours and then skim off the fat and strain. Put the boiled macaroni into a saucepan with a piece of butter, plenty of grated Parmesan cheese, and as much of the gravy as it will absorb ; toss it on the fire a little and then serve.

Sparghetti may be used instead of macaroni.

Lasagnes aux Tomates à la Napolitaine.
Macaroni à la Napolitaine.

Mince half a pound of fat bacon together with a clove of garlic, a couple of onions, some parsley, thyme, marjoram, and basil to taste, till it becomes a paste, when place it into a saucepan with one *pound of fresh* beef cut up into small pieces.

Keep on turning this on the fire till the meat is well browned, then moisten with a little stock, and add the contents of a bottle of conserve of tomatoes. Let this simmer for an hour, put in pepper and salt to taste, and if it be too thick add more stock; then strain it carefully, remove superfluous fat, and put by till wanted. Take half a pound of the broad flat macaroni called lasagne (though the long kind can be used), break it into lengths, and throw it into a saucepan of boiling water, with some salt. Keep stirring, but be careful not to break it. The moment it is done pour into the saucepan a jug full of cold water. Strain immediately. It takes about half an hour to cook it. Place it on a deep dish with a few pieces of fresh butter, then arrange the lasagne in layers, pouring plenty of the sauce with a good sprinkling of grated Parmesan over each. Put more butter on the top, more sauce, and plenty of Parmesan. Put in meat sauce in front of fire for ten minutes, and serve.

Macaroni with Tomato Sauce.

Macaroni à la Sauce Tomate.

Boil a pound of Naples macaroni with a piece of fresh butter the size of an egg, an onion, two cloves, and some salt; when done, drain the macaroni, and place it in a saucepan with five ounces of grated Gruyère cheese, five ounces of Parmesan cheese, some black pepper, and six tablespoonfuls of cream; toss over the fire until the cheese becomes thick and stringy. Dish up in a pyramid and mask with thick tomato sauce.

Savoury Rice.

Riz aux Délices.

Put into a saucepan six cupfuls of stock or broth into which has been previously dissolved a good allowance of either tomato paste or tomato sauce; add pepper and salt to taste; when it boils, throw in for every cupful of stock half a cupful of rice, well washed and dried before the fire. Let the whole remain on the fire until the rice has absorbed all the stock; then melt a large piece of butter, and pour it over the rice.

Semolina Canapés.

Goulez de Reyna.

Take one pint of milk, one ounce of butter, and two ounces of semolina. Boil to a thick paste, and then add one ounce of Parmesan cheese. Lay on a dish till cold, then cut it into fingers, egg and crumb them and brown in the oven. Serve with good gravy round.

Savoury Vermicelli.

Vermicelli à la Venise.

Boil one pint of milk; when boiled, put in three tablespoonfuls of vermicelli. Let it simmer for five minutes, then add three eggs; beat up all together with a gill of cream, salt, white pepper, and a small shalot.

Butter a mould and stick it all over with small neatly cut pieces of ham and tongue. Pour in the mixture. Then bake it, and serve it, when turned out, with savoury gravy or tomato sauce.

Tongue Toast.

Grate finely the remains of a tongue and mix it with the yolk of an egg or a spoonful of cream, finely chopped parsley, pepper, and salt. Make it very hot (but not boiling), and pour it on to fingers of well-buttered hot toast; sprinkle thickly with fine bread-crumbs, and let them brown before the fire.

Gascony Butter.
Beurre de Gascogne.

Take two ounces of parsley, two ounces of anchovy paste. First boiling the parsley, pass it through a sieve till quite fine, then mix the parsley, anchovies, and two ounces of butter together. Make it up into balls and put it on ice till it is time to serve it with the cheese.

Montpelier Butter.
Beurre de Montpellier.

Pick the leaves of a quantity of watercress, mince them as finely as possible, and dry them in a cloth. Then mince them still more and dry them again. Then knead them with as much fresh butter as they will take up, adding a very little salt and pepper.

Work it up into balls, and serve with the cheese course.

Artichoke Bottoms à la Käiser.

Cook some artichoke bottoms, season them with a little grated Parmesan cheese. Choose some plain, round, glossy tomatoes and place one on each artichoke ; lay some mushroom purée on the top of each, taking care to smooth it well ; place each arti-choke on a fried croûton mashed with the tomato purée, and put them in a deep tin dish and bake them in the oven (which must not be a fierce one) for about ten minutes. Just before serving sprinkle a little finely-chopped parsley over, and curl an anchovy on the top of each round a spray of parsley that has been heated in the oven.

Fried Artichokes.

Artichauts Frits.

Cut the artichokes into slices lengthways, remove the chokes, cut off the tops of the leaves, trim the bottoms, wash them in vinegar and water ; drain them, and dip them into a thin paste made of eggs, flour, cream, pepper, salt, with half a wine-glass of brandy. Fry in oil or lard. Serve with fried parsley sprinkled with salt.

Stewed Artichokes.

Fonds d'Artichauts.

Strip off the leaves from the artichokes, remove the chokes, and soak them in tepid water for about three hours, changing the water occasionally. Place them in a saucepan with enough gravy to cover them, a tablespoonful of mushroom ketchup, the strained juice of a lemon, and a piece of butter the size of a walnut rolled in flour. Let them stew gently till tender, then serve with the sauce *poured* over as hot as possible.

Stewed Artichokes with Essence of Ham.

Artichauts à l'Essence de Jambon.

Trim the artichokes, cut out the chokes and stuff with minced mushrooms, minced bacon, parsley, and shalots, which have been cooked in butter.

Line a braising-pan with slices of bacon, add the artichokes, season with pepper and salt, and a bouquet of mixed herbs; moisten with half a pint of stock, and cook over a slow fire with hot coals on the lid.

When done, dish up, covered with essence of ham, which is made by mincing some ham very fine, pounding it and warming it in melted butter; then stir in a very little flour, and moisten with a little stock. Season with a bouquet of herbs, minced mushrooms, and a teaspoonful of vinegar, pass through a sieve, and pour over the artichokes.

Stuffed Artichokes.

Artichauts Farcis.

Thoroughly wash the artichokes. Boil them till nearly tender, drain them, remove the middle leaves and the chokes, and lay in each a little good forcemeat, and put them in a moderate oven until the meat is sufficiently cooked. Make a good rich brown gravy to serve with them.

Any kind of forcemeat may be used.

Artichokes à la Lyonnaise.

Artichauts à la Lyonnaise.

Cut up the artichokes into quarters, remove the chokes. Put them into a saucepan with some

melted butter flavoured with lemon juice, simmer
till done ; then take out the artichokes, and add to
the sauce a teacupful of stock, a piece of brown
thickening, two or three slices of onion, and a bit
of butter the size of a walnut, and leave on the fire
to brown ; then pass through a sieve, season with
pepper and salt, and add a teaspoonful of chopped
parsley.   Warm the artichokes in this sauce, and
serve.

Jerusalem Artichokes à l'Italienne.
Artichauts à l'Italienne.

Wash and peel the artichokes, shaping them
like pears of uniform size.   Butter a stewpan with
two ounces of butter, and arrange the artichokes in
circles.   Strew over some pepper, salt, and lemon
juice ; pour a quarter of a pint of good gravy over
them, put the lid on, and simmer for half an hour,
basting them occasionally.   They should colour a
deep yellow.   Serve with cream sauce or Italian
sauce round them.

The Italian sauce is made with a quarter of a
pint of white stock, a wineglass of Chablis, which
must simmer till reduced to one-half ; add a few
finely minced mushrooms, one shalot, a bouquet of
thyme, and parsley.   Thicken with flour and butter,
and stir over the fire three minutes ; then simmer
for a quarter of an hour, stirring slowly.

This dish can be varied by sprinkling them with grated Parmesan.

Asparagus Omelet.
Omelette aux Pointes d'Asperges.

Boil about twenty-five heads of asparagus, and
cut the green ends when tender into short pieces.

Mix with them four well-beaten eggs, adding a little pepper and salt.

Melt an ounce of butter (or perhaps rather more) in an omelet-pan, pour in the mixture, stir till it thickens over the fire, fold it nicely over.

Asparagus sauce may be served with it, or clarified butter into which a few drops of vinegar have been poured.

Asparagus with Cream.
Asperges à la Crème.

Cut up some heads of asparagus, wash and drain them, boil them for three minutes, and simmer for half an hour ; drain again, and stir some clotted cream into them, and serve in a glass dish.

Asparagus à la Pompadour.

Boil the asparagus in boiling salt and water. When cooked, cut it into lengths of about three inches, drain them, and let them lie before the fire for a few moments. Then take one ounce of fresh butter, two yolks of egg, a pinch of salt, a salt-spoonful of pepper, and a tablespoonful of vinegar. Cook in a saucepan till thick ; dish up the asparagus in a pyramid, and pour the sauce over.

Beetroot Fritters.
Betteraves à la Chartreuse.

Cut some boiled beetroot into slices. Take two pieces at a time, place a slice of raw onion sprinkled with chopped chervil, pepper, and salt, between them, dip into batter, and plunge into boiling fat. When a good colour, dish up.

Broad Beans with Cream.
Fèves de Marais à la Crème.

Take the smallest and youngest of the beans and throw them into boiling water for a few seconds (if old, they must be skinned). Boil them in a pint of milk, with two ounces of butter, a dessertspoonful of chopped parsley, and a pinch of salt ; thicken the sauce with two whipped yolks of egg, and stir in two tablespoonfuls of cream.

Omelette au Cresson.

Beat up three eggs in a half a pint of water with salt and pepper to taste.

Take the middle of two shalots, a little watercress, and a few tarragon leaves. Mix the herbs thoroughly together, add them to the eggs whilst beating, and make the omelet in the usual way.

Omelet of French Beans.
Omelette aux Haricots Verts.

Cut up finely two tablespoonfuls of French beans, stir into them four well-beaten eggs ; then add two tablespoonfuls of grated Parmesan, with a little pepper and salt to taste. When perfectly mixed, put the whole, with two ounces of melted butter, into the omelet-pan, and fry a pale brown. *The time varies* from three to five minutes.

Omelette à la Jardinière.

Stew some minced mushrooms, carrots, turnips, French beans, herbs, young green peas, and broad beans in stock. When done, stir in a little brown thickening ; take half the vegetables, beat together with twelve eggs, and cook the omelet in the usual manner. Serve covered with the remainder of the cooked vegetables.

French Beans à la Poulette.

Haricots à la Poulette.

Take tender French beans, remove all fibres by breaking off the ends ; wash and boil them in boiling water. When done, toss them in melted butter seasoned with chopped chives and parsley ; stir in a dessertspoonful of flour, a pinch of salt, and a quarter of a pint of stock ; reduce the sauce, thicken with three yolks of eggs, and flavour with a few drops of lemon juice when it is ready to serve.

Cauliflower Fritters.

Marinade de Chouxfleurs.

Blanch the cauliflower and break it into pieces, dip into a thick béchamel sauce, and leave it till it is quite cold ; then take each piece separately and dip into batter made of a half a pound of flour and one ounce of melted butter mixed in a bowl ; stir well, and, when the paste is perfectly smooth, moisten with just enough warm water to make it a proper substance, to which a pinch of salt is added and the whipped white of an egg. After dipping the pieces of cauliflower in the batter, fry in boiling lard or butter. Serve hot, garnished with fried parsley.

Cauliflowers au Gratin.

Chouxfleurs au Gratin.

Take a nice white and close cauliflower, and cut away its outer leaves. Put it head downwards in a saucepan with plenty of fast-boiling water slightly salted, and let it boil till tender ; it must be kept with the flower under water. All scum must be removed as it rises. When it is done take it up and drain it on a sieve, then place it on the dish it is to be served in, and squeeze it together gently in a clean cloth, and a sauce poured gently over it made of two ounces of grated Parmesan cheese, half an ounce of butter, an ounce of flour, a quarter of a pint of cold water, a tablespoonful of cream, and a grain of cayenne pepper. The cream should not be put in till the sauce is well boiled, thick, and smooth, and the cheese should be stirred in last. Sprinkle some grated cheese on the top and brown it with salamander.

Cucumber with Eggs.

Pare three large cucumbers, cut them into small squares, and put them into boiling water. Take them out of the water and place them in a stewpan with a small onion, a piece of pork, and a lump of butter and a little salt. Keep them on the fire covered close for a quarter of an hour, sprinkle with flour, and add sufficient veal gravy *or light stock* to cover. Stir well together, and keep a gentle fire until no scum will rise. Then take out the pork and onion and add the yolks of ' two eggs and a teaspoonful of cream. Stir for a moment, take off the fire, and squeeze in a little lemon juice. Have ready four or five poached eggs to lay on the top.

Stuffed Cucumbers.

Concombres Farcis.

Cut two cucumbers into slices about two inches thick, but do not use the ends; peel and remove all the pips, scald them for ten minutes, plunge them into cold water and drain them; line a china fire-proof dish with slices of bacon cut thin, stuff the cucumber rings with forcemeat composed of some veal finely minced without gristle, and fat from the calf's kidney; season with salt, pepper, and a grain of grated nutmeg, moistened with a wineglassful of milk, and pound till quite smooth. Having filled the rings of cucumber with this forcemeat, wrap them up in slices of bacon, which tie round with a string; moisten with a pint of stock, and bake for twenty minutes in a slow oven. When done, drain the cucumber, take away the slices of bacon and dish up, covered with a sauce made of a quarter of a pound of butter, one ounce of flour. Brown it and moisten it with stock; add a little glaze, and stir over fire for twenty minutes; pass through sieve and flavour with lemon juice.

Stuffed Cucumbers à la Roma.

(Italian recipe.)

Take some fresh cucumbers, hollow them out partly by taking out the middle where the seeds

E

are.   Make a mince of chicken or veal mixed with
a little forcemeat, chopped tomatoes and butter
(it should be a soft mince); fill up the cucumber
with this, and cork up the ends with pellets of
bread or dough.   Stew them gently in a brown
gravy, to which add the insides of the cucumbers;
the pellets of bread must be taken out before
serving.   Dish them up on long fingers of fried
bread with the sauce made over them; the sauce
should be thickened.

Cucumber Mayonnaise.

Put the beaten yolk of an egg into a basin with
a very little salt, pepper, and cayenne, and a teaspoonful of lemon juice; mix these to a cream, and
then add a few drops at a time some best olive oil,
and stir till thick.   A little more lemon juice will
thin it, and then add more oil, proceeding on this
alternate mode till half a pint of oil has been used.
Grate a fresh peeled cucumber till there are about
three tablespoonfuls of it, and beat this into the
mayonnaise.   Fry some filleted sole in egg and
bread-crumbs, and serve the cucumber mayonnaise
with it.

Morels à l'Andalouse.
Morilles à l'Andalouse.

Cut half a pound of ham into dice; fry them
in salad oil, and, when a good colour, put in some
morels; moisten with half a pint of sherry, a gill
(quarter pint) of Madeira, season with a mixture
composed of a saltspoonful of salt, half a teaspoonful
of pepper, and a teaspoonful of capsicum powder
to which add a dessertspoonful of finely-minced
parsley.

Cook all this for forty-five minutes; dish up the morels in a pyramid and pour the sauce over them, which must be thickened with flour and flavoured with lemon juice.

Mushroom Baskets.

Paniers de Champignons et Tomates.

Make some puff paste; roll it out *very* thin; line some small moulds with it, filling up the centre with barley that they may keep their shape till baked, when it must be removed. Fill the inside of these moulds with mushrooms and tomatoes minced; pound this mixture in the mortar with a small shalot, one ounce of butter, a tablespoonful of thick white sauce, into which a few drops of lemon have been squeezed.

Some of the puff paste should have been twisted into lengths bent to the shape of handles, and baked at the same time as the puff paste. Put the handles in, and decorate with fried parsley and preserved barberries.

These baskets can also be filled with lobster, chicken, or game.

Mushrooms au Gratin.

Champignons au Gratin.

Chop up half a dozen mushrooms and mix them in a stewpan with an ounce of lean ham, grated, and the same quantity of the fat of bacon, scraped. Add pepper and salt to taste, and a saltspoonful of minced thyme; let all these fry together for a few minutes, then add the yolks of two eggs, stirring them all together till cooked. Prepare some large flat mushrooms by peeling and trimming the

E 2

edges and cutting off the stalks. Fill each with some of the above preparation, and cover with raspings of bread ; spread butter thickly over and place the mushrooms in the sauté-pan and sauté them. Next put them in the oven for a quarter of an hour, till brown. Dress these, when done, in a pyramid, and serve a good brown sauce round them in which has been boiled a tablespoonful of chopped mushrooms, a tablespoonful of chopped shalots, and a bay-leaf ; then strain into the dish. A glass of Chablis mixed in the sauce is an improvement.

Mushroom Jelly.

Gelée aux Champignons.

Take a couple of pounds of mushrooms. Put them in a stewpan with a gill (quarter pint) of mushroom ketchup ; squeeze in a few drops of lemon into which a little pepper has been mixed. Melt in a gill of water half an ounce of gelatine, and strain it. After the mushrooms are sufficiently soft, pass them through a sieve, add the strained gelatine, and pour the mixture into a damp mould ; when turned out, decorate with finely chopped aspic. A few of the very small tomatoes might be parboiled to decorate the top of the jelly. This jelly looks very pretty made in small dariole moulds and simply garnished with aspic.

Mushroom Omelet.

Omelette aux Champignons.

This omelet is made like any of the preceding. *The mushrooms* can be chopped up in the egg mixture, or can be made into a purée, and inserted between the folds of the omelet after it is folded.

Mushroom Scallops.

Coquilles aux Champignons.

Take mushrooms, peel them and soak them in lemon juice. Have ready a white sauce into which half a lemon has been strained, and add a mustard-spoonful of mushroom ketchup. Take the soaked mushrooms and stew them slowly in this sauce, and, when tender, pour them into scallop shells ; cover with bread-crumbs, place pieces of butter on the top, and brown them with a red-hot salamander.

Stuffed Mushrooms à la Lucullus.

Champignons Farcis à la Lucullus.

Wash, dry, and trim the mushrooms ; chop up the stalks with a teaspoonful of minced parsley and tomato, and warm this mixture for a few moments in some butter. Fill the mushrooms with this mixture, place them on a buttered baking-dish and bake them about six minutes, basting them with clarified butter.

This dish may be varied by sprinkling over the tomato a little grated Parmesan cheese.

Mushrooms and Tomatoes.

Champignons aux Tomates.

Toast a slice of bread, butter it, and cut it into rounds two inches in diameter. Dip the tomatoes into hot water and peel them ; cut them into thick slices, and lay them on the toast ; on the top of these place a peeled mushroom. These must be put into a buttered tin, and a little clarified melted butter poured over each ; then place the dish into the oven for two minutes, and baste them whilst cooking. Serve hot and quickly.

Olives with Anchovies.

Olives aux Anchois.

Take some Spanish olives and stone them ; wash and fillet four anchovies, and mince them finely, also a quarter of a teaspoonful of minced onion, a little chopped parsley, and a grain of red pepper. Put this preparation inside each olive in place of the stone, put them on the croûtons, and serve with mayonnaise sauce.

Olive Custards.

Talmouses d'Olives.

Take one ounce of grated Parmesan cheese to one egg well beaten up, mix this over the fire till it becomes a very thick custard ; fry some neat little rounds of bread in butter, spread them very thinly with anchovy paste, and pour on each a small quantity of the custard. Stone some olives, and put one in the middle of each round.

Stuffed Olives.

Olives Farcies.

Make small rounds of fried bread, run water-*cress butter* round them, here and there making a pattern. The olives must be turned—that is, peeled, as if they were pears; fill each with sardines, lobster, or anchovies; place alternately with these in the dish pieces of caviar on fried bread, squeeze some lemon over all, and ornament round the fried bread with run butter.

For Watercress Butter, *see* under that head.
To run butter is to squeeze it through cones or bags made on purpose, and sold at all ironmongers'.

Onions à la Wolsey.

Take a Portugal onion and cut a thick slice from the root end. Place it in boiling water and parboil it and fill it with a mixture of pork sausage-meat and mashed potatoes in equal parts; add the yolk of an egg. Have ready a small piece of broiled ham and place under the onions; add a good brown gravy and stir them quickly and serve.

Onions au Gruyère.

Boil some medium-sized onions, toss them in butter a few moments and then pour over them a thick white sauce, into which two ounces of grated Gruyère cheese has been added.

Onions al Vino.

Slice and peel two large Spanish onions, cut them into rings, sauté them in butter for five minutes over a very clear fire; drain them and put them into enough Chablis to cover them; next add an ounce of fresh butter rolled in flour. Sprinkle upon them a dust of cayenne, pepper and salt to taste, and cook them slowly and serve with little sippets of toast under them.

Stuffed Onions.

Oignons Farcis.

Take a large Spanish onion, scoop out the centre, peel and blanch it ; fill the centre with force-meat, and place it in a stewpan ; cover it with slices of bacon, sprinkle with salt and sugar, and cook over a quick fire.   When done, remove the onions, reduce the sauce and pour it over them, and serve.

The forcemeat can be made of chicken, ham, parsley, and mushrooms, and some chopped suet, all finely minced together with pepper and salt to taste.

Potatoes à la Milanese.

Take as many potatoes as are required.   Choose the largest, *bake* them well, then cut off the tops and scoop out the insides.   Pass the potato through a sieve and add a tablespoonful of grated Parmesan and Gruyère cheese mixed, pepper and salt.   Melt two tablespoonfuls of butter in a stewpan, put in the potatoes and make it hot ; fill the potato cases with it, put them in the oven for a few minutes, and serve up very hot.

Potato Ribbons.

Pommes de Terre en Garniture.

Wash and peel the potatoes, taking out the eyes and specks ; peel them as you would an apple, very *thinly* into ribbons ; place them in a frying basket and fry them in boiling fat for about six minutes. Sprinkle with salt. Dish them in a pyramid on a napkin.

Potatoes à la Parisienne.

Pommes de Terre à la Parisienne.

Chop up a pound of onions very finely, and brown them in equal quantities of butter and lard. When a good colour, moisten with a quarter of a pint of stock; add a pound of mashed potatoes, season with a bouquet of herbs, salt, and pepper. Serve very hot on a napkin.

Potatoes à la Provençale.

Pommes de Terre à la Provençale.

Mash two pounds of potatoes, pass them through a wire sieve, season with pepper and salt. Grate two ounces of Gruyère cheese, and pound it in the mortar with enough butter to make a paste; add a quarter of a pint of milk and a little minced parsley. Put this into a frying-pan, stirring in the potato, and fry till of a pale brown. Dish it up high, *en pyramide.*

Potato Scallops.

Coquilles de Pommes de Terre.

Mash two pounds of cold potatoes with milk and pass through sieve; add three ounces of butter melted, two ounces of grated Parmesan cheese, pepper and salt to taste.

Fill some scallop shells with this mixture and brown them in the oven. Whilst hot, glaze each over with melted butter and one ounce of grated cheese; hold the hot salamander over to brown them.

Parmesan Potatoes.

Pommes de Terre au Parmesan.

Take some large potatoes, bake them; cut off a round piece on the top of each. Scoop out the potato, mash it with butter, pepper, salt, and grated Parmesan cheese, and refill the skins and heat them up in the oven.

Pumpkin à la Parmesan.

(Italian recipe.)

Clean and peel a pumpkin, let it stand in salted water, drain it, put it in a pan on the fire with butter, suet, and spices. Let it fry, stirring it constantly; afterwards add another piece of butter and some grated Parmesan cheese; put the lid of the saucepan on, and let it roast with fire above and below it.

Neapolitan Savoury.

Make some salad dressing (*see* under Lucullus Salad Dressing), mix with it some aspic jelly (half a pint) to half a pint of salad dressing; divide it into four parts, leave one as it is. Colour and flavour one with tomato purée, one with mushroom purée, and one part colour green only. Have ready some little Neapolitan ice paper cases, fill these with layers of the different salad dressings (of course, each layer must be set before the other is put in); chop some aspic and sprinkle over the top, and serve with it some vegetable or fish sandwiches *cut in oblong* shapes.

Savoury Omelet.
Omelette aux Fines Herbes.

Break two eggs in a basin, whip them, adding pepper and salt to taste. Mince finely a small piece of shalot and a teaspoonful of parsley. Melt some butter in the omelet-pan, and when quite hot pour in the eggs, and proceed as for all other omelets.

Spinach Fritters.
Beignets d'Epinards.

Boil spinach thoroughly, drain and mince it well ; add some grated bread, one grate of nutmeg, and a small piece of sugar. Add as much cream or yolks and whites of eggs as will make the preparation of the consistence of batter ; drop the   . batter into a frying-pan of boiling lard. When the fritters rise, take them out, draw, and send to table.

Fairy Tomatoes.
Tomates aux Fées.

Take six or eight fair-sized tomatoes, cook them till tender with a shalot, a dust of cayenne, then pass them through the sieve, adding a little stock, in which a tablespoonful of ketchup has been mixed ; then take the lean part of a veal cutlet, one ounce of lean ham, pound it and pass it through a sieve, and then divide it equally in half ; then add with it half of the tomato purée, adding the yolk of an egg ; then butter a mould and place in the pure tomato purée, then the pounded veal and ham, then the mixed tomato and veal, dividing the mould into three parts. Steam this for half an hour,

taking care not to boil it ; when ready turn out of
mould and serve with white mushroom sauce. This
may be eaten cold with aspic jelly and slices of
tongue stamped in rounds as garnish.

Tomato Canapés.
Canapés aux Tomates.

Cut some slices of bread two-and-a-half inches
in diameter and one-eighth of an inch thick, fry
them a pale colour, and spread them when cold
with Parmesan butter (that is, butter and grated
Parmesan cheese well pounded together). Dip
small tomatoes into hot water, skin them and put
one on each piece of bread, arranging some finely
minced parsley around and grated Parmesan on
the top of each.

Tomato Jelly.
Gelée aux Tomates.

Take two pounds of tomatoes, half a grain of
red pepper, and two shalots. Place them in a stewpan, and boil them till quite soft. Melt fifteen
sheets of the thin French gelatine, and pour it into
the mixture, then pass all through a sieve, and
mould. Serve with chopped aspic jelly. A little
grated Parmesan sprinkled over it is an improvement.

This savoury can be made in the same manner
with one pound of mushrooms and one pound of
tomatoes.

Tomato Omelet.

Proceed as for oyster omelet, using minced
tomato instead of oysters, into which a small piece
of shalot and a pinch of cayenne has been mixed.

Tomatoes en Surprise.

Take half a pound of well-washed rice, pour to it a quart of boiled water, adding a teaspoonful of salt ; cover it and let it boil till the rice is quite tender, then throw it into a colander to drain. When well drained, if not quite ready for use, put it into a saucepan, cover to prevent drying, and keep hot. Pour the juice from fresh tomatoes, stew them a short time, season them with plenty of butter, pepper, salt, sugar, adding a small grated onion. Just before sufficiently cooked add enough bread crumbs to absorb most of the juice ; butter a mould thoroughly, and line it with the cooked rice nearly an inch thick, and let it stand for ten minutes where it will keep hot without drying. Just before serving fill the mould with the tomatoes, cover with rice, then turn all out from the mould and serve. It should look very firm and white ; a sauce à la Morny should be served with it, which is a white sauce with grated Parmesan, and should look like custard.

Tomatoes à la Mauritian.

Take away the peel and seed of two very large tomatoes, and add to the pulp one-third the quantity of finely-chopped chives, a tablespoonful of cream, a third less of lemon juice, a little salt, and two or three chilies shredded, and, if in season, a little shredded celery. Next mince and pound to a paste some oysters ; to this add gradually some finely chopped chives, two or three chilies, salt, salad oil enough to make paste like butter, and then a dessertspoonful of lemon juice. Prawns, shrimps, lobster, anchovies, or sardines may be used instead of the lobster.

Stuffed Tomatoes.

Tomates Farcies.

Dip as many tomatoes as required into boiling water for a minute, peel them ; make a hole near the stalk, scoop out the centre of the tomato with an egg-spoon, and place them on a buttered or oiled sheet of paper in a baking tin.

Make a stuffing with sausage meat and very thin tomato sauce ; fill the tomatoes with this, sprinkle over with grated bread-crumbs, and place a piece of butter on the centre of each. Bake for ten minutes in a good oven ; dish them on fried croûtons and serve quickly.

Stuffed Tomatoes à la Financière.

Tomates Farcies à la Financière.

Dip the tomatoes into boiling water, peel them and scoop out the centres with a small spoon, and place the tomatoes on a tin dish. Mix a lump of butter the size of a walnut with one ounce of flour, a little mushroom liquor, a tablespoonful of tomato sauce, a dessertspoonful of olive oil, a teaspoonful of chopped parsley and shalots in equal quantities, a little salt and pepper to taste ; stir all in a stewpan till quite hot and *thoroughly* mixed. Fill each tomato with some of this stuffing, sprinkle them with grated bread-crust. Pour a few spoonfuls of olive oil into the dish, and bake for ten or *twelve minutes,* and brown with a salamander.

Tomatoes Stuffed au Gratin.

Tomates Farcies au Gratin.

Cut the centre from six tomatoes all of uniform size, and squeeze the pieces cut without breaking them ; season each with a very little salt and pepper. Mince six mushrooms, chop finely one onion, two shalots, two ounces of lean ham or tongue, and about a teaspoonful of parsley. Put all these chopped ingredients into a small stewpan with two ounces of butter, and stew well over the fire till they are thoroughly cooked, taking care not to burn them. Have some brown sauce ready, which stir into the other ingredients.

Fill each tomato with some of this preparation, and sprinkle over each some bread-crumbs in which has been mixed a dessertspoonful of grated Parmesan cheese ; put a small piece of butter on each. Place them in a moderate oven for about ten minutes, and serve quickly and hot.

Tomato Timbale.

Timbale à l'Andalouse.

Boil half a pound of macaroni till tender but not broken, strain it, and cut it into lengths which will fit a plain round mould ; line the mould with it, arranging the top by bending the macaroni in a spiral form. Fill this timbale or mould with a mixture made of one pound of tomatoes, one pound of mushrooms, and a quarter of a pound of grated Parmesan cheese, all pounded together with four ounces of butter and the yolk of an egg ; season with a teaspoonful of salt and a grain of red pepper.

Put a paper round the mould, leaving two inches standing above the edge of the mould, and steam it for an hour. Turn out, and ornament it with very small tomatoes on the top, and serve with mushroom sauce round it.

Minced truffles and lobster spawn rubbed through a sieve and sprinkled all over it gives it a very nice appearance.

Broiled Truffles.
Truffes sous la Cendre.

Wash and peel the truffles, roll each in a thin slice of bacon, season with a very little salt and pepper; cover each one with four pieces of paper which have been dipped in cold water; bury the truffles in hot cinders and leave them for a quarter of an hour, after which remove the first two pieces of paper and serve.

Iced Salad à la Fascination.

Take two or three large heads of white celery, cleanse it, and chop it very finely; take a small Spanish onion, parboil it, also a small shalot. Pound them up thoroughly and mix all together, pound and pass through a sieve. Take some beetroot, cut it up in *very thin slices*, also some watercress (choose very green leaves), mince small, pound and pass through sieve; if not a very bright colour add a little green colouring. Make a mayonnaise sauce with a dessertspoonful of Swiss milk, the yolks of two eggs, and beat them up together; then add a mustard-spoonful of made mustard and three drops *of essence of* anchovies; pour in some salad oil drop by drop, then a tablespoonful of tarragon vinegar, then more salad oil, then a tablespoonful of cream, and add half a pint of whipped aspic jelly and whip up all together.

Oil a fancy mould and place at the top a little clean aspic jelly, which place on ice to set. Mix some of the mayonnaise sauce *well* into the onion and celery mixture, let the beetroot slices soak in some and colour a little green and mix into the pulped watercress.

When the aspic jelly in the mould is set place a layer of the watercress an inch and a half thick ; then when that is set add a similar sized layer of the celery and onion mixture ; then add when set a layer of the slices of beetroot, and when that is set fill in with the rest of the celery and onion mixture ; leave on ice till fit to turn out ; garnish with mounds of aspic decorated with chervil leaves alternately with small tomatoes.

Salad Sauce Lucullus.

(Original recipe.)

Take a full dessert-spoonful of Swiss condensed milk, a mustard-spoonful of made mustard, the yolk of an egg, six drops of anchovy sauce, and a pinch of salt. Work all these well together, and when quite smooth add a quarter of an onion, pounded fine, which well stir in. Then pour in half a teaspoonful of Worcester sauce, half a tea-spoonful of chili vinegar. After blending these together, add a gill of salad oil drop by drop, beat it up well in the sauce, then pour in a teaspoonful of tarragon vinegar, drop by drop, and finally six tablespoonfuls of salad oil, drop by drop, well whisking all the time.

Brittany Salad.

Take a couple of potatoes, a good thick slice of beetroot, and three onions. Boil the potatoes and bake the onions and let them get cold. Cut the beetroot into thin slices and arrange all these in a circle, alternately a slice of each. Put a heap from a tin of macedoine of vegetables (draining them first) into the middle. Pour oil and vinegar over them and serve.

Potato Salad.

Salade aux Pommes de Terre.

Bake some potatoes, peel, slice, and place them in a salad bowl with two or three onions cut into quarters and two wineglassfuls of claret ; stir until thoroughly mixed, then season with salt and pepper ; add a little vinegar, and *plenty* of oil. Put in two or three chervil leaves minced very fine ; stir till thoroughly mixed.

Potato and Truffle Salad.

Salade de Pommes de Terre aux Truffes.

Bake, peel, and slice some potatoes. Cut up some truffles which have been boiled in white wine into very thin slices, and arrange them in alternate layers in a salad-bowl with the sliced potatoes ; the last layer must be of truffles. Garnish with small pickled onions, fillets of anchovy, and either stoned or stuffed olives ; sprinkle with salt and pepper. *Mix* a dressing of oil and vinegar, and pour over.

Orange Salad (for wild duck).

Remove all the skin and pith from the orange, cut it into its natural divisions, and season with salad oil, brandy, a teaspoonful of castor sugar, and the same of finely-chopped tarragon and chervil.

Red Cabbage Salad à la Russe.

Salade de Choux Rouges à la Russe. ˋ

Cut up a red cabbage into very fine narrow strips, plunge for a minute into boiling salt and water, cool in cold water, drain, lay in a deep dish and sprinkle with salt and tarragon vinegar.

Stir some mashed hard-boiled yolks of egg into half a tumblerful of sour cream ; season with salt, pepper, chopped chervil, and tarragon leaves. Pour over the cabbage, and garnish with a few slices of black radish.

Russian Salad.

Salade Russe.

Chop up some cold fillets of chicken and par-tridge with carrots, turnips, and asparagus, all of which have been cooked ; take some cold boiled peas, small French beans, beetroot cut into lozenges, crayfish tails, capers, stoned olives, and fillets of anchovy ; stir all these ingredients thoroughly to-gether, and add a little caviar, a pinch of cayenne, a minced shalot, black pepper, mustard, oil, and vinegar.

No particular flavour ought to predominate in this salad, therefore it requires that the ingredients be perfectly mixed.

ʀ 2

Tomato Salad à la Duchess of Fife.

Chop up some tomatoes quite small, flavour them with a bead of garlic and a shalot chopped and rubbed through a sieve, which mix in with the tomatoes; add four tablespoonfuls of whipped aspic jelly, and mix into the purée with the same quantity of mayonnaise sauce. Decorate a mould with hard-boiled eggs stamped out in fancy rounds and stars, and arrange them in tiers one above the other. Between each layer of egg place a leaf of chervil and a sprig of tarragon alternately. Fill the mould with the tomato purée, place on ice, and when ready turn out. Garnish with small salad mixed with mayonnaise sauce round the base, arrange watercress prettily on the top, and sprinkle chopped aspic all over it.

Vegetable Salad.
Salade de Légumes.

Boil equal quantities of carrots, peas, asparagus heads, French beans, potatoes, and half the quantity of turnips; when done, drain carefully and place in a salad-bowl in separate groups, with a head of boiled cauliflower in the centre. Cover with a sauce made of twelve tablespoonfuls of salad oil, two of vinegar, half a teaspoonful of anchovy sauce, a little salt, pepper, an idea of cayenne, and a rub of garlic, and stir well.

Winter Salad.
Salade d'Hiver.

Shred celery and onion very fine. Pour over *it mayonnaise* sauce. Stand watercress upright in the centre. Place beetroot cut in rounds all round the edge alternately with quarters of hard-boiled eggs.

This salad should be served on a flat dish, and not in a salad-bowl.

Anchovy Sandwiches.

Tartines d'Anchois.

Soak anchovies in milk, after boning them (unless they are already boned). Spread them on bread and butter, with a layer of cress.

Anchovy and Egg Sandwiches.

Tartines à la Chasseur.

Pound anchovies and hard-boiled yolks with butter. Place between slices of bread and butter, with a layer of watercress.

Caviar Sandwiches.

Tartines à la Caviar.

Spread caviar on bread and butter, squeeze lemon over it, and add a trifle of cayenne pepper.

Chicken Sandwiches.

Tartines à la Reine.

Take cold chicken, cut it into very delicate thin slices, pour over it a good béchamel sauce, and make into sandwiches.

Cucumber Sandwiches.

Tartines aux Concombres.

Cucumber cut in slices and dressed with either vinegar and oil or salad dressing makes very exquisite sandwiches in the summer.

Curry Sandwiches.

Tartines à l'Indienne.

These sandwiches are made with either curried eggs or fish of any kind.

Egg and Chutnee Sandwiches.

Tartines à la Pondicherry.

Pound hard-boiled eggs together in a mortar with a little chutnee, and make into sandwiches.

These can be made with piccalili pickle instead of the chutnee.

Latcore Sandwiches.

Bouchées Latcore.

Take three anchovies, washed and pounded, with a small piece of ham and chicken. Make a very good curry sauce, and mix all together. · Stir over the fire till nearly boiling. Fry small rounds of bread, and spread mixture on them. Serve hot with a little grated cheese (mixed with butter) on *the top.* Heat for five minutes before sending up.

Lobster Sandwiches.

Tartines au Homard.

Pound lobster with a little anchovy butter, and make into sandwiches.

Shrimps and prawns may be used instead of lobster.

Lobster and Egg Sandwiches.

Tartines à l'Amphitrion.

Pound lobster, egg, and butter together with a trifle of cayenne and one or two capers, and make into sandwiches.

These may be also made with shrimps or prawns.

Tartines de Gibier.

Ptarmigan and game sandwiches are also very appetising sandwiches.

Mushroom Sandwiches.

Tartines aux Champignons.

Stew the mushrooms, squeeze a little lemon over them, adding a trifle of pepper and salt, and make into sandwiches.

Mushroom sandwiches may be likewise made with equal parts of mushrooms and tomatoes.

Mustard and Cheese Sandwiches.

Tartines à la Jardinière.

Take some Gruyère cheese, mince it finely; add some made mustard and make into sandwiches.

Oyster Sandwiches.
Tartines aux Huîtres.

Take large stewing oysters, pound them in a mortar with a little cayenne and lemon juice; spread them on thin slices of brown bread and butter and cut them into shape.

Parmesan and Egg Sandwiches.
Tartines au Parmesan.

Pound the yolks of eggs with butter and grated Parmesan and make into sandwiches.

Pâté de Foie Gras Sandwiches.
Tartines au Pâté de Foie Gras.

Buy some tinned pâté de foie gras, make sandwiches of it. A small piece of aspic jelly put on the foie gras is a great improvement.

Radish Sandwiches.

Cut some round radishes into very thin slices, and mince finely the best part of the green leaves. Put the latter in a cup, and slightly moisten with vinegar and a little sugar. Then take several slices of thin bread and butter and spread the radishes and leaves on them.

Salad Sandwiches.
Tartines à la Printanière.

Make a nice salad, mince it small; add the dressing and make into sandwiches.

Salmon Sandwiches.
Tartines au Saumon.

Cut slices of salmon and cucumber, and put them between bread and butter and roll them up in a lettuce leaf soaked in vinegar for an hour, or in salad dressing.

Sardine Sandwiches.
Tartines aux Sardines.

Wipe and bone the sardines, squeeze a lemon over them ; place them inside the bread and butter with a layer of cress.

Sardine Sandwiches à la Mayonnaise.

Bone the sardines, pound them well; add mayonnaise sauce, and place them inside the bread and butter.

Tomato Sandwiches.
Tartines aux Tomates.

Skin the tomatoes, cut them in slices ; add a few drops of anchovy sauce and make into sandwiches. Or the tomatoes may be skinned and masked with mayonnaise sauce and made into sandwiches. They can also be made with sliced tomatoes and grated Parmesan cheese.

Victoria Sandwiches.

Cut slices of brown bread and butter, bone and clean sardines ; spread them on the bread and butter with some mustard and cress on the top. Cut into sandwiches.

INDEX.

PRINTED BY
SPOTTISWOODE AND CO., NEW-STREET SQUARE
LONDON

WS - #0189 - 300924 - C0 - 229/152/5 - PB - 9781330471944 - Gloss Lamination